Going to Seed
Dispatches from the Garden

Going to Seed

Dispatches from the Garden

Charles Goodrich

Silverfish Review Press
Eugene, Oregon

A number of these dispatches were first published in the following magazines: *Moving Mountain, Northwest Review, Origin, Windfall,* the online journal *Terrain* and in a chapbook: *Heavy Mulching: Eleven Dispatches from the Garden* (Knot House Press, 2008). Gratitude is due to the editors and publishers.

Cover art: *Suspicious Aroma* © 2002 by Yuji Hiratsuka
Woodcut: *Storm Crow* © 2009 by Aaron Goodrich
Woodcut: *Crocus* © 2010 by Aaron Goodrich

First Edition

Published by

Distributed by

Silverfish Review Press
P.O. Box 3541
Eugene, OR 97403
www.silverfishreviewpress.com

Small Press Distribution
800-869-7533
spd@spdbooks.org
www.spdbooks.org

Library of Congress Cataloging-in-Publication Data

Goodrich, Charles, 1951–.
  Going to seed : dispatches from the garden / by Charles Goodrich. --1st ed.
    p. cm.
ISBN 978-1-878851-58-1 (alk. paper)
I. Title.
PS3607.O592254G65 2010
811'.6--dc22

2010001072

Manufactured in the United States of America

for Kapa and Elliot

and everyone with hands in the Earth

Contents

Now I am terrified at the Earth, it is that calm and patient,
It grows such sweet things out of such corruptions

–Walt Whitman

The day is coming when a single carrot, freshly observed,
will set off a revolution.

–Paul Cezanne

I. Summer

Truck Garden

My first wife and I rented a little bungalow in the center of town. We were young. Our furniture was nothing but apple crates.

The backyard butted up to a Ford dealer. There was a wall of new pickup trucks at the end of our garden. We planted everything we could dream of, even rutabagas. She had sweet peas climbing the downspouts; I grew peanuts in buckets on the back porch. She brought home two kittens, Basil and Sage, but they both died and we buried them under the juniper.

Before anything was ripe, the Ford guy bought the place, evicted us, bulldozed the house, and paved the yard. Thirty years later, I still think of those cats buried under that asphalt. And who knows what else.

Temporary Burial

All I did was stick a zinnia behind my ear. Then the kids decided to cover me in flowers. My son tucked cosmos and snapdragons in my collar. His little friends piled sunflowers on my lap, jammed chrysanthemums up my sleeve, stuffed a dandelion into each nostril.

It was like being buried in sand, playing dead for the amusement of the children. Sometimes I like acting helpless. And little kids can be such imaginative tyrants.

But of course they quickly tired of the game. And I was left sitting in my lawn chair, indistinguishable from the garden, visited only by bees.

Drip

The nurse swabs antiseptic on my knee. It smells like spinach
with lime. My empty stomach rumbles. "Hungry are we?" she asks.
I can't see whether she's smiling behind her mask, so I stare right into
her eyes, and she stares back.

The first time they reamed out this knee, I watched it on the
video screen. The bone was whiter than teeth. There was hardly any
blood. The surgeon told us his favorite marinade for grilled snapper—
lemon, paprika, and ginger—while his tiny pneumatic scissors
trimmed my meniscus.

Now the anesthesiologist slides an IV needle into my arm.
"What'll it be this time—the epidural or the full monte?" Suddenly
I remember—I left the drip irrigation running in the garden. Shit.
Too late to call home. If the potatoes get scab, I'll kick myself.

Global Warming

Too hot for June. The sky feels thin, and the sun is much too close. What am I doing out here anyway, lips chapped, eyes stinging, sweat-soaked before noon?

I'm unclogging nozzles, that's what! Setting sprinklers, hooking up soakers, dragging hoses around the yard. Who could have foreseen a heat wave this soon?

At least the artichokes are happy, their armored hearts clenched tight in spiny scales. If we let them flower, they'll open into monstrous blossoms, purple ogres with bumblebees in their nostrils. But we won't let that happen. We're going to cut off their heads, and eat them.

The Behavior of Flies

I've always thought they were good-for-nothing free-loaders, trash mongers, corpse defilers. Even the adults were just winged maggots, to my mind.

But this one on the porch rail appears to be doing exercises—push-ups, neck stretches and wing-flexing isometrics. Which makes sense when you think about it, for what is the fate of an out-of-shape fly?

Its wings are like isinglass. It has bulbous eyes the color of chestnuts, and whenever I lean close, it crouches and holds still, ready to flee if I move to strike. And I am tempted to take a swat—it's a kind of itch in my chest muscles, an urge to lash out.

River Midges

That's what I'd do if I were one of them—glide up and down like that in a tight column with a hundred of my kin, cruising intently beside the river as if there were no tomorrow, all of us small and drab, no social climbers among us, no bosses or peons, just an unremarkable middle-class family of insects out for a late-summer evening's swarm.

From time to time one of the midges leaves the dance, and veers away to course over the water. I've done that, flown away and come back, sadder, maybe wiser. And now two midges grope in mid-flight, a quick insemination, and I shiver in sympathy.

Yes, nothing better of a summer's evening than being a midge. If anyone questions your worth, tell them, hey, I wasn't born yesterday. Indeed, I was born this very morning. Look around—every moment is an eternity. Give no thought for the morrow, for there shall be none.

Among Birds

I'm walking the lower path, worrying about a friend with breast cancer, when I hear a slight sound—the flutter of quick wing beats. I stop and hold still. Soon a flock of tiny birds riffles through the trees. Bushtits. Each bird just a feathered heart-beat, a hot-blooded little wish.

They are gleaning something from the buds of the trees, insects perhaps. They toss their simple words back and forth—*tseep, tseep*—scratching their necks, stropping their beaks, close enough I could almost touch them.

My friend is adept at being among birds, making a quiet place inside her. One time, three goldfinches perched on a branch just above her, and she whispered, "Do you think they know how happy they are?"

Fertilizer

At six, he already suspects that I'm the Tooth Fairy, that it's my hand that wriggles under his pillow, snitches the bloody little tooth, and leaves him a coin or two.

But he doesn't have a clue what I do with his teeth. I don't let him see me bury them in the rose bed. He may be getting a little old for cozy superstitions, but he's still too young for organic chemistry.

I will do anything this side of the grave to keep him safe. But as for his teeth—calcium, phosphorous, protein—they're going back to the earth.

Teepee

I cut seven bamboo poles and tie them together at the neck, then spread their feet around the bean hill and push each pole deep into the ground. Strung with twine, it's a trellis, and a secret.

Later, when the beans have climbed the poles and grown a skin of green over the teepee, I hide inside, watching the honeybees sip at the bean flowers. The chickadees don't know that I'm spying on them as they pluck the seeds from my sunflowers. Wary of our dog, but ignorant of me, the neighbor's tabby pads through the lettuce.

My wife leans out the back door and calls a name. It used to be my name. But not today.

The Master

Early morning in the garden, I'm watching a bumblebee bang around in a poppy. He buzzes over to a penstemon, shoves his way down a blossom, then backs out with pollen stains on his face. Now he shambles across the rosemary like a drunkard and stumbles onto an aster, a clumsy, fat ballerina in a black tutu.

It's hard to take this bumblebee seriously, with his stubby wings, pudgy thorax, geodesic eyes. When he lifts his ponderous body in flight, he fudges several laws of aerodynamics. If this is how plants get pollinated, it's a wonder the planet survives. Weird, how evolution flirts with absurdity.

My mother used to tell me, "Don't be half a fool." So I bow to the bumblebee, my mentor in accident and indirection, who has gotten himself stuck just now in a foxglove. Humming and shoving, he shimmies back out, waggles his butt and buzzes away, the master, my implacable guru.

A Distant Relative

A tiny leather pouch, with six legs, and a wicked assortment of surgical tools in its mouth—it's a tick, clinging to my sock. A simple, blood-sucking bag of appetite, and a generous purveyor of Rocky Mountain spotted fever and Lyme's disease. Its face looks rather like a hole-saw.

We are distantly related, I suppose, if you go back far enough, back to some inconceivably remote common ancestor, like, say, my great-aunt Aggie's great-great-uncle, Amos Grabill, the family's legendary parasite.

Amos came home from prison camp at Chancellorsville toothless, emaciated, one-eyed, and crazy, and built himself a tiny cabin at the back of the farm. He wouldn't help with the field work after the war, the story goes, just wandered the pastures all day chanting poems to the sheep, and he died young, and childless.

Concrete Buddha

His meditation garden has all the right parts: clipped azaleas, Japanese maples, a tiny moss-shouldered pond. Even a patch of raked gravel with three nice granite boulders sticking up.

No koi in the pond, though. A great blue heron ate them, he tells us, coming back from the kitchen with glasses of iced tea. And, no, he doesn't spend that much time out here. His import business is taking off, and he isn't home as much as he'd like to be.

We sip our tea, admiring the tranquility of the scene. But I can't help noticing that the life-size statue of the seated Buddha, painted a weathered-bronze green, is tilted several degrees out of plumb, a posture that would be painful to maintain.

Scar

The big garter snake basking beside my wheelbarrow is an old acquaintance—I recognize it by the nasty scar on its side. Its sleek body has a bulge halfway back, the yellow pin-stripe broken by a dark lump with no scales.

I gave it that wound. Harvesting spuds last summer, I turned up a forkful of new potatoes and one writhing snake. I'd nicked it with a tine of the spading fork.

It looks peaceful enough sleeping in the sun, but I'll bet that wound still aches. Of all the garter snakes that live in our yard, this is the only one I know on sight. I wish it weren't so, but I never forget the creatures I have hurt.

Surge

Glen says his corn is growing so fast he can hear the leaves swelling in the night. I don't believe him. But I go out into my garden after dark and sit on a pumpkin and close my eyes.

I'm a good listener. I can often hear things that aren't even happening. But tonight, though I notice the wheezing of cars in the distance, and a forlorn squawk from some sleepless bird, I can't hear a peep out of the corn.

The quiet gets thicker than fog, and I almost drift off. But finally I hear a soft, watery surge, like distant surf. It could be the aquifer flowing beneath our place. It could be satellites feeling for the pulse of space. It could be the soil itself, alive and breathing, or the wireless warbling of human desire. Or it could be the corn.

Spirit Mountain

Tedious, mind-numbing, hard on the knees—weeding carrots is a chore I hate. My blunt fingers are just no good at it—groping the foliage, trying to distinguish carrot from weed. The shoots of the Chantanays are interwoven with bedstraw and chickweed, so for every weed I pull I also uproot healthy baby carrots.

According to my friend Harry, the invention of agriculture was the beginning of the end. Once we domesticated plants and quit hunting wild game, we settled down to the business of getting fat, and the rest is history: drug-laced beef, cardboard apples, industrial chickens, and the soybean deserts of the Midwest.

He might be right. After crawling on my knees for most of an hour, back aching, fingers cramping up, I begin to daydream that I'm on the hunt. This carrot is my atlatl. I crouch behind the elderberry and whisper my song, stalking an elk below the mountain called Tcha-tee-man-wi.

Another Futile Raid on the Ineffable

Full summer. A gorgeous, warm, dewy morn. Hoping to be struck dumb by wonder, I go out to the garden and stand agog—hands loose at my sides, gaze unfocused, lips parted just slightly—a willing instrument for revelation. But nothing happens.

A chickadee hangs upside down on a sunflower, prying out seeds with its beak. The pumpkin vine has grown a foot overnight, but now it just rustles its leaves as if shaking off the dew. A hummingbird probes the honeysuckle with its ordinary zeal. Nothing more.

My cheeks are tired of smiling. My patience is almost drained. The mysterium has failed me again. Nothing wondrous occurs, not even a whiff of awe. The shadow of a single cloud passes over the bell peppers, narrowly missing me.

II. Fall

Crow

Still thinking about that crow I saw flying over the park this morning. He kept stalling in mid-flight and falling a couple of feet before he would flap his wings and fly again. And he was crying out, over and over, in a wretched, faltering voice.

You know those crow calls—the grouchy command, the simpering whine, the gargle, the shout? Well, this was different, full of heartbreak or woe. If he were my friend, I'd be worried about him.

Eco-Tourism

I lift a slab of half-rotted lumber at the edge of the garden, and find myself in a teeming bug metropolis, as if I'd stepped off a train in a city where I don't understand the language.

Centipedes, like articulated buses, cruise into freeway tunnels. A gang of ants hustle little white eggs into underground alleys. Sow bugs, a fleet of gray taxis, weave in and out of traffic. The soil itself seems to be moving, like a city sidewalk crawling with pedestrians.

Suddenly I realize it's getting late. I need to find a room for the night. Where the hell am I anyway? Does anyone here speak English?

An Ant in the Gorge

Sitting by my campfire in the Columbia River Gorge, with the hiss and pop of burning cedar punctuating the drone of traffic on I-84, I think about the catastrophic floods that roared through here ten thousand years ago when the ice dams that held back ancestral Lake Missoula fractured and burst, carving those stair-stepped striations in the walls of the Gorge and gouging coulees out of solid basalt in the Channeled Scablands north of here—cataclysms of unimaginable scale.

"Geology makes me feel insignificant," I tell the ant climbing my shin. It's a big carpenter ant, its feelers tapping my leg hairs, tarsal hooks pricking my skin. I intercept it with a finger and it scrambles onto my palm and keeps on trucking. I block its path, making it clamber from hand to hand, again and again, forgetting for a minute how small and lonely I am.

Then the ant plunges off my knuckle and disappears into the duff. And I'm left alone, staring into the fire, thinking about floods, earthquakes and tsunamis yet to come.

Ground Zero

After a friend phones to tell me—*Two planes*, she says, *right into the Towers*—I grab my gloves and head straight to the garden. In the corn patch only a few sad ears remain. I yank them off, then chop the stalks and dump them in the compost bins. Where the lemon cucumbers have sprawled between the corn rows, I find overgrown fruits, hard and dark. I lob them toward the bins, feeling a twinge of satisfaction when I hear one hit a post and burst open.

I tug too hard at the carrot-tops and they tear off, so I dig the carrots out with the spading fork. Carrots sprawl in the dirt like startled fish. I pull up two rows of bush beans and knock the earth from their roots. Dry seeds rattle in the overgrown pods. I strip one open with my thumb, and stuff a few black seeds in my pocket.

The lettuce plants have all bolted. I rip off a leaf of romaine and the stem oozes milky fluid. I take a bite—it's bitter. I eat it, and eat one more. Suddenly weary, I wash the tools and put them away, brush the leaf-mold from my jeans. I've skinned a knuckle somehow. As I suck at the dirt and blood, a squadron of crows—seven or eight of them—drop into the garden to scavenge what's left.

All Saints' Day

We only got nine trick-or-treaters last night. The rain blew sideways, and wind snuffed out the jack-o-lantern's candle. By the time the kids made it to our house, the witches, pirates, and princesses all bore a sodden similarity.

Rain, rain, rain, but still no frost. The garden isn't going to freeze this year—it's going to drown. Restless indoors, I pull on my raincoat and go out to work. The skeleton of a sunflower has toppled face down in the mud. A dozen unpicked tomatoes are just empty pouches of blotchy pink skin. What seems a dead rat is only the final zucchini furred with mold.

I start pulling up the blighted beans, but my gloves are quickly slimed. When I try to pitchfork the pumpkins into the wheelbarrow, they slump into pulp. Rain is trickling down my neck. My boots are slick with putrefaction. The hereafter is here and now, maybe, but there's mud on my glasses and I can't see it.

Cold Soil

November 7, 2004

I'm listening to the latest returns on the radio. The country seems bent on re-electing Greed. To salvage the hour, I break up my garlic, slitting the skin around the neck with a paring knife, pressing my thumbs in beside the stem, prying out one clove at a time. As I drop each clove into the bowl, I mutter a string of prayers and curses—breaking up garlic as an irreverent rosary.

I have to plant this garlic before dark. The moon is not right, the weather is against me, but I need to put my hands in the dirt today. I need to sow something. I'd be smarter to wait a few days until the rain lets up, but I can't wait. Some things can only be sown into coldness.

I pry open another head, and another, praying to the Earth to transform my anger into compassion. Or at least into garlic.

Black Friday

Deep in the brambles, a winter wren scavenges insects for her supper, talking to herself in buzzing little syllables. Otherwise, things are quiet in the woods.

It's the day after Thanksgiving, signs everywhere of recent feasting. Beside the river, a scrubby willow has been clipped off, the clean impression of beaver teeth indented in the stump. At the base of a cedar, a fresh owl pellet, chock full of white bones and gray fur. And here, in the center of the trail, splayed out in artful array, the scrub jay's wings sail on through a scatter of gray and blue breast feathers, right where the fox left them.

I'm sure it will be a busy day at the mall. There are supposed to be bargains galore. I can believe it, because the catkins of the wild filberts are already an inch long. And now the wren flits to a branch above the trail and scolds me for undisclosed offenses. Prosperity abounds!

Shade Garden

Sit down, she says, pointing a bony finger toward the lawn chair. She hands me a cup of coffee, and lowers herself onto the rusted, wrought-iron loveseat.

I used to grow dahlias, you know. It's too shady now, but twenty years ago there was quite a bit of sun back here. We kept this apple tree pruned down, and that cherry wasn't there—the birds planted it around the time my husband died. I can't keep the yard up anymore, but I like it this way, going back to the wild.

I had the boy dig out my roses. They had black spot and aphids, and hardly bloomed. Even the grass has given up—you can see it's mostly moss on the ground. Nothing else will grow, but that's fine. All I really want now is shade.

Under the Ivy

Once, at the Convent, dumping leaves into the wooded ravine, I dropped my rake down the steep, ivy-covered slope. When I went to retrieve it, my boot struck something under the ivy. I cut away some vines, and found terra cotta pots, the crumbling remains of a wrought iron bench, and a foot-high ceramic statue of the Virgin.

This must be the place Sister Josephine told me about. In the early years of the Cold War, the convent got a hundred new novices a year. Many were just off the farm, and they wanted a bit of garden to ease their loneliness and fear. The Mother Superior told them to pray to Jesus, but she also gave them this shady, good-for-nothing woods to potter in.

They cleared out the ivy, terraced the slopes and transformed a hundred yards of ravine into a garden. They lugged in boulders to make the little creek jump and sing. Summer evenings they held vespers down there—I found their brick fire pit overgrown with ferns. Think of it: a hundred young women in black wimples gardening in the ravine.

Night Soil

They've built a new composting outhouse here at Waldo Lake. The old pit toilet up in the forest had a better view, but this one's clean and almost odorless. I approve. If I see a ranger I'll ask what they do with the final product.

Night soil—isn't that a lovely name for excrement? For forty centuries, Chinese farmers composted it and returned it to their fields. High in minerals, phosphorous, nitrogen, it's safe to handle if you cook it right.

When I worked at the Convent, we composted the sludge from the sewage treatment plant to fertilize the trees and shrubs. Nun dung, we called it. The roses bloomed profusely, and the rhododendrons grew immense.

Garden Noir

Damn. The squashes have crossed again. This one is supposed to be an acorn squash, but it looks like a billy club with warts. How far apart do I have to keep these plants? Some vegetables have no shame.

And look at this: tell-tale spots on the tomato leaves. Under my pocket magnifier, pretty yellow rings with dead tissue in the center. Necrosis, caused by who knows what—a virus, a fungus, a mutant pathogen. Probably infectious. Better rip up the whole lot before it spreads to the peppers.

Listen, you've got to be tough to grow vegetables. Tough, smart, and a little bit mean. Because plants are headstrong and narcissistic, prey to all the sins of the flesh. They'll strangle each other when you aren't looking. Make no mistake—in the quest for food, beauty, and truth, a lot of creatures are going to get hurt.

Music to Garden By

Bobby's playing his squeeze box on the porch next door. Somebody farther off is mangling blues chords on a badly tuned electric guitar.

I'm pulling up overgrown carrots and beets, grunting and sighing—that old animal music—sometimes humming along with Bobby's Irish ditties, sometimes with those hapless blues.

And sometimes I just pause, sit back on my haunches and listen to the breeze sawing at the leaves of the apple tree, the wing-beats of the chickadees hurtling past me, or the steady hum of the earthworms eating the ground beneath my feet.

III. Winter

Black Tomato

Even before I'm fully awake, my skin registers how cold the house is. Cold moonlight seeps in around the closed curtains. The cold world's little sounds are frost-muffled, too—the ticking of lumber shrinking in the walls, scritch of bamboo against the windows, thud of a car door down the street.

I am coldly pleased. Autumn has limped on too long, the garden sputtering out tasteless tomatoes, bitter bell peppers, tough-skinned crooknecks. Weary of harvest, fed up with stoop-labor, I still feel duty-bound to eat everything—cracked radishes, beetle-bitten green beans, the final slug-riddled cabbage. I want the whole garden executed.

I bundle up and go outside. The garden is flocked. Every surface of leaf and stem is furred white with a fine-woven, tightly-fitted shroud. I snap a frozen tomato from a vine. As it thaws in my hand, I squeeze it to mush.

The Boss

Hard freeze overnight. Frost gloves every twig and grass blade. The trees stand shivering all day in an icy fog. Finally, late in the afternoon, the fog slinks back into the sky, and I maunder out to the garden.

It looks like a garbage dump out here. The dog has been hauling rubbish out of the compost, littering the grass with squash rinds and coffee filters. Dead tomato vines hang in their wire cages. Along the west side of the garden, there's a big sheet of black plastic smothering the ground. I put it there to kill the grass, to make next year's garden even larger. Now the plastic is puddled with rainwater, green and slimy and doodled with drowned worms.

The plastic stops at the water spigot, and next to the spigot sits the skeleton of an aluminum lawn chair, nylon webbing in tattered shreds. It's the boss's chair, the overseer of death and decay. Though he's so busy he never sits down.

Going to Seed

January evenings, I sit by the fire, salivating over the latest
fashion magazines—Burpee's, Wayside Gardens, Johnny's Selected
Seeds—dreaming that I'm still a young stud, still up for double-
digging a new bed, getting it on with the latest hybrids.

Once I was biodynamic. I used to do a lot of heavy mulching.
I tried my hand at companion plantings, played around with French
intensive. There was a time I'd dibble seed into any dirt I came
across.

But I'm done sowing wild oats. I'm not planning to graft a
branch on some other guy's tree. Anyway, who cares who can raise
the biggest zucchini. I'm happy just looking at the pictures.

Face Down

I dream I have dropped dead, smack in the garden. I'm face down in the mud, in the rich, dark, much-amended loam. Surprisingly, I really don't mind when the ants crawl over my eyeballs, when the centipedes wriggle into my crevices. It seems fitting that earwigs can finally access my ears.

Some of my favorite writers—Ed Abby, Lew Welch— disappeared into the wild. They wanted to re-enter the food chain without detours. And I am drawn to those photos of Tibetan morticians hacking up corpses on rocky outcrops, feeding the meat to magnificent vultures.

Of course, I'm not in any hurry. And I want to be thoroughly dead when they eat me. Not just this creeping, incrementally dead—fungi colonizing my toes, a virus camped out in my lungs, my mind being slowly digested by the acids of daily life.

The Milky Way

Agitated by this evening's quarrel, unable to sleep, I slip out of bed, tug on my clothes and step outside. A hard frost has fallen, and the neighborhood is eerily silent, as if the frost were sucking up all sounds.

The sky is very clear. The stars of the Milky Way flicker and pulse. They seem to be saying something difficult in the slowest possible cadence. After a while, I can't recall what she said that so angered me.

Maybe love doesn't need to be willed, only not impeded. I want to wake my wife and ask her to forgive me, but I just crawl back into bed and lie beside her, shivering.

Live Music at Christmas

Cold fog all morning, a frigid chill that penetrates the bones.
I take the dog outside, throw a stick for her, twice, then even she's
ready to go back indoors. Now, with my chair drawn close to the
woodstove, I read and daydream while the wet dog steams at my feet.

I prefer my Decembers quiet and slow, but my son wants a
boom box for Christmas, and soon I must get up and shop. The
prospect of canned music at the mall is benumbing. For a while
longer I put it off, listening to the laundry rolling in the clothes dryer.

Then, from outside, I hear something like a sick crow. Or
what is it? A thin croak, like a twig dragged over a wash board. Again,
and once again, and I'm beginning to understand. I go back outside,
and sure enough, there it is, clinging to the underside of a sword fern,
a tree frog, singing in the warmth from the clothes dryer vent. Hark
and rejoice!

End of December

They are planting their potted Christmas tree in the front yard. Dad and the young daughter dig the hole, the girl leaping on the shovel with both feet. The day is gray and cold, but Dad has worked up a good sweat, and Mom, bouncing an infant in her arms, says something to the girl, and laughs.

The Douglas fir is only as tall as the girl, and green as deep summer shade. Wisps of tinsel twinkle from its limbs. For the next few years, they will string it with lights and garlands of cranberries for the birds. By the time the girl finishes high school, the father's tall ladder won't reach the top, and they'll give up decorating it for Christmas.

You have to admire them, setting this tree loose in their small lawn. You have to believe that this little ceremony will serve them well, when the parents are old and the tree has heaved their sidewalk and darkened their windows, when they lie sleepless, stiff with fear, as the tree limbs groan and scrape at the roof on a stormy December night.

The House of February

On the far side of the river, there's a grove of old cottonwoods, ragged trees with storm-splintered crowns. Some have toppled into one another's arms, and all are bare now in early February. Here and there in the crotches of the branches, the canopy is clotted with big, messy baskets—nests of the great blue herons.

When the trees begin budding in another month, the birds will return, carrying sticks as long as their beaks. They'll line the nests with feathers and moss, lay clutches of eggs, and hatch their naked, ungainly chicks.

But today, I don't want to think about eggs, or hopes, or starting over. I just want to savor the desolation of those trees, the slate sky, the empty nests.

IV. Spring

Mudding-in Peas

Courting the muse is not like sowing peas. You can sit quietly all through February, pencil in hand, quivering with attention for hours on end, and you may or may not be given a poem. But you sure won't grow any peas.

For peas you must leave your desk, step into your boots, and go out to the garden. You will be on the cusp of winter, a bite to the air, the soil barely awake. Hard to believe any seed would want to be sown this early.

But now your faith in the muse pays off. Your long apprenticeship to whatever happens prepares you to believe in the genius of a pea. The seed is ready. And you are ready to assist it. And you have a pencil, perfect for dibbling the holes.

Small Engines

They have carried my neighbor's tilt-up bed into the living room so he can watch the outside world go by. A couple of his grandkids have planted a pressure-treated four-by-four in the front yard, mounted a new birdfeeder, and filled it with sunflower seeds and millet.

Twenty years we've lived next door to one another. Have we ever once talked about birds? Only the weather, or sometimes the inner workings of small engines.

The hospice lady has just left. Chickadees flock to the new feeder. I can see my old friend gazing out his window. I've known him so little, hardly at all. How very strange to be here now, in our separate lives, watching the same birds.

Beans

They've built a vault in Svalbard, Norway, buried inside a mountain above the Arctic Circle—a bunker for seeds. Temperature-controlled, access limited, built to withstand a nuclear bomb, it's a doomsday repository for germplasm.

Meanwhile, here in Corvallis, Shari's taking the opposite strategy. She's handing out bean seeds to everyone in the neighborhood. String beans, pinto beans, kidney beans, favas. Grow these, she tells us. Grow more than you need, and share them with strangers. Save some for seed and pass them along.

I take my share, and promise to spade up another bed. But seriously, how many beans can one person eat? I guess time will tell. And if things get really bad—sea-levels rising, plague, famine, war—it's nice to know there's a stash of seeds in Svalbard, Norway.

Garage Sale Ecology

Whenever I cross paths with Maynard, he's filling his old VW with cinder blocks, short lengths of lumber, plastic flower pots, scraps of fencing, bags of baler twine—the dregs of everybody's garage sales—stuff he uses for building raised garden beds in his backyard. He feeds at the bottom of the garage sale food chain, and always finds plenty.

Me, I'm usually looking for something specific: a left-handed tin snips, a throttle cable for my rototiller, or a pump sprayer that hasn't been used for pesticides. Most days I come home empty-handed, my time wasted.

I thought about Maynard last night as I listened to a biologist talking about climate change, how plants and animals here in the Willamette Valley may respond. The generalists, she told us, will likely adapt and thrive. The specialists are going to have to migrate or die.

Erosion

These little gullies the rain has carved in the slopes of my carefully raked garden bed—they remind me of the wrinkles around my grandmother's eyes. Also the scar on my brother's chest where they tucked his heart back in.

Water carves away earth. Surgeons carve away flesh. Even stone flows—I've watched molten rock as it squirmed into the ocean, hissing. But the squirrel that got run over in front of our house this morning never made a sound.

A garden isn't the cosmos, just one of its dreams. I hoe the gullied soil back onto the bed, scatter some old straw on top, and the erosion is temporarily undone. But what about that dead squirrel? When I buried it under the blueberry bushes, three crows gabbled in the walnut tree, grumbling at the waste of a good meal.

Interstition

Sticking to ritual makes things tick. Ask the robin sitting on her nest. Ask the lilacs beginning to bud. Ask me. Or better yet, take this shovel and help me plant these spuds. You dig the trench and I'll set a seed potato every two feet in the row.

Because it's St. Patrick's Day, and that's when we plant potatoes. The college boys down the street are celebrating another way, playing ping pong in their driveway puking drunk, because they know as well as you and I do that famine is just one blight away. While they put their faith in cheap revelry, I'm paying court to the old dirt gods, burying these spuds with a prayer they'll let me stay another year above-ground.

You might think it's superstition, but it's actually *interstition*, acting on blind faith that the individual things we see are all stitched together by something potent and invisible. Better not ask what it is. Just dig.

Lettuce

Into each cell of the egg carton I tamp an egg's-worth of soil, then press into each seed-bed three seeds. I spritz them with tapwater, and place the carton on the windowsill above the kitchen sink.

A week later, the seedlings have arisen, every one. Twelve groves of tiny plants, each sprout just a pair of seed-leaves on a slender pinkish stem, succulent and alert.

But now I hesitate. If I really want full heads of lettuce, I have to thin these plants, have to pick up the scissors and kill two of each three. In the everlasting tussle between spirit and matter, no one knows when his time is up. I feel the blade at my own neck.

Feng Shui Cowboy

Raw energy swoops in this window behind my desk and swirls around these piles of books like a flock of barn swallows circling a silo. Then it cyclones past the lamp, bounces off the computer, and splinters into a hundred unruly forces like wind through a sieve. Loose threads of energy rummage through the mail, disarrange my files, erase names from my memory. A side-channel riffles constantly through the dictionary.

Sometimes energy arrives in a torrent, overflowing all my efforts to contain it. Other times, it sputters in feeble spurts, as if some spiteful deity had shut the tap.

Either way, my job is to wrangle these wayward currents onto the page using just this pencil. A Chinese sage probably does it silently, with great presence of mind, but I'm more likely to cuss or whoop.

Report from Behind

At the age of thirty, I vowed to cultivate patience. At forty, I decided I wanted nothing more than time. So I took my time, and now I'm fifty, and I've fallen far behind—no job, no cell phone, no implants, not a single tattoo.

I don't know the names of the latest pop stars or even the current Pope. When it comes to trivia games, I'm a total loss. I couldn't tell you who won the World Series or the war in Iraq. I'm just a straggler, an aimless pilgrim, a student of the weeds beside the road…

Say, look here—it must have rained last night. The dust has settled. The bloom is back on the cheeks of things. The thistles are almost ready to pop. I don't suppose I will ever catch up.

V. Summer
Again

New Flag

Atop the dead cedar at the edge of the cemetery, a turkey vulture basks in the late-morning sun, wings stretched wide to capture the heat. There's also a girl in a lavender bikini sunbathing on the mausoleum lawn. I hope she's using plenty of sunscreen.

I keep the dog on the leash, and walk briskly along. Funny, I still can't decide whether I want to be buried or cremated. They say if it weren't for buzzards, the whole world would be knee deep in rotten meat.

I look back and see that the girl has turned over, limbs splayed out like a corpse. And the vulture is preening, combing greasy feathers through its beak. If the country wanted a new flag, I'd vote for that bird—patient, charitable, with a highly developed sense of smell.

The Wind in the Trees

The old trees along the street are reveling in the afternoon breeze. A trio of black walnuts, some tall cottonwoods, the lone Siberian elm. The fluttering of their leaves makes a purring sound like a stream pouring over gravel. The leaves rustle and gleam like moving water. I could watch them forever.

Though in fact my attention wanders. Sitting here in the shade, unbidden images flit through my mind—my father standing beneath a willow, fishing for bluegill in Tennessee; my mother in a little sailboat at Lake Minnetonka, waving to me on the shore. The rustling leaves and restless images intermingle.

What if my thoughts aren't merely mine? What if consciousness wafts through the leaves and the folds of the mind? The breeze picks up and the trees all sway. The trees seem to be doing the moving, the images seem to play behind the eyes, but it's really the wind, or something within the wind, that's causing all the stir.

The Garden of Forking Paths

A peony blossom can trigger it, or a stalk of bamboo bent low with rain. Suddenly I'll get the strangest feeling that I have been in this exact place before. How on Earth did I get here? What path lies ahead?

Today it's a yellow rose my wife placed on our nightstand. Though it's been there for days, I've barely noticed. But now it's all I can see. Faded to a pale sunset, almost ready to drop its petals, I know I've been in its presence some other time.

I have a photo of my mother holding me, an infant six days old. She looks haggard and thin, her curls are limp. I know that she almost died in delivering me. On the nightstand beside her, there's a pack of Lucky Strikes, an ashtray half-full of butts, and a single rose in a narrow vase. I am just a lump in her lap, a nose and eyes peering out of a blanket. Now I sit on the bed and gaze at the two roses. When the first petal falls, I want to be here.

Wild Blackberries

That first summer, we went to her secret patch by the river. In the heat of late August, we picked two heaping buckets, then pelted each other with oozing fruit. She put blackberries on my tongue, and I painted her cheeks with purple juice. Back at her house, we made blackberry jam, the kettle steaming until the windows ran, and we slept holding each others' purple hands.

But now that we are older, blackberries are the enemy. Briars overwhelm our fences, infest the orchard, overtake the fields. Everywhere we look, the countryside is plagued with brambles.

The thickets of age are constricting our hearts. Is there still time to go blackberry picking once again?

Sun Struck

Slaughtering weeds in the afternoon heat, hoeing and raking, stooping and tugging, I suddenly get light-headed and nauseous, feel like I'm going to faint. I lie down in the path beside the tomato cages, my heart thumping, sweat pouring off my face.

From the house, I hear my son calling—"Dad!"—and now he's standing at the end of the row, looking down at me. He's fourteen, often embarrassed by my uncool ways. And yet he's still just a boy, with a fuzz of adolescent beard, and a shadow of worry on his face. "Dad, are you okay?"

My head has quit spinning, my heartbeat is back on pace. From down here I can see dozens of green tomatoes the size of walnuts dangling from the vines. "Yeah," I tell him, "I'm okay. I'm just working on my tan." I'd like to rest here a little longer, gathering courage from those hard, green fruits. But he reaches out his hand, and I let him haul me up.

Calico

Sixteen years old and crippled with arthritis, she couldn't have weighed more than a half gallon of milk. Her cloudy eyes oozed a milky fluid. We talked about putting her down, but if you scratched her behind the ear, she would purr until she couldn't catch a breath. And she'd still hobble over to the dish for her kibbles.

This morning, I found her on her pillow, cold and empty, lighter than a bird. My wife wrapped her in a scrap of wool tartan, and I went to dig a grave between the lilacs. My first shovel of earth came up full of new potatoes, the size of eggs.

I know nothing about the transmigration of souls, but I made potato salad for supper, and we talked about what kind of bird a cat might become.

Wild Geese

I'm picking beans when the geese fly over, Blue Lake pole
beans I figure to blanch and freeze. Maybe pickle some dilly beans.
And there will be more beans to give to the neighbors, forcibly if
necessary.

The geese come over so low I can hear their wings creak, can
see their tail feathers making fine adjustments. They slip-stream along
so gracefully, riding on each other's wind, surfing the sky. Maybe
after the harvest I'll head south. Somebody told me Puerto Vallarta is
nice. I'd be happy with a cheap room. Rice and beans at every meal.
Swim a little, lay on the beach.

Who are you kidding, Charles? You don't like to leave home
in the winter. Spring, fall, or summer either. True. But I do love to
watch those wild geese fly over, feel these impertinent desires glide
through me. Then get back to work.

About The Author

Charles Goodrich is the author of a previous volume of poems, *Insects of South Corvallis*, and a book about nature, parenting, and building his own house, *The Practice of Home*. He has also co-edited *In the Blast Zone: Catastrophe and Renewal on Mount St. Helen*. His poems and essays have appeared in many magazines including *Orion*, *The Sun*, *Zyzzyva*, and *Best Essays Northwest*. A number of his poems have been read by Garrison Keillor on *The Writer's Almanac*.

In a long career as a professional gardener, Charles has taken care of the grounds of a convent, a school for wayward youths, and an historic county courthouse. He presently serves as Program Director for the Spring Creek Project for Ideas, Nature, and the Written Word at Oregon State University. He lives and gardens with his family near the confluence of the Marys and Willamette Rivers in Corvallis, Oregon. www.charlesgoodrich.com.

This book was set in Adobe Jenson, a faithful electronic version of the 1470 roman face of Nicolas Jenson. Jenson was a Frenchman employed as the mintmaster at Tours. Legend has it that he was sent to Mainz in 1458 by Charles VII to learn the new art of printing in the shop of Gutenberg, and import it to France. But he never returned, appearing in Venice in 1468; there his first roman types appeared, in his 1470 edition of Eusebius. He moved to Rome at the invitation of Pope Sixtus IV, where he died in 1480.

Type historian Daniel Berkeley Updike praises the Jenson Roman for "its readability, its mellowness of form, and the evenness of color in mass." Updike concludes, "Jenson's roman types have been the accepted models for roman letters ever since he made them, and, repeatedly copied in our own day, have never been equalled."

Silverfish Review Press is committed to preserving ancient forests and natural resources. We elected to print *Going to Seed: Dispatches from the Garden* on 30% post consumer recycled paper, processed chlorine free. As a result, for this printing, we have saved: 1 tree (40' tall and 6-8" diameter), 385 gallons of water, 155 kilowatt hours of electricity, 42 pounds of solid waste, and 83 pounds of greenhouse gases. Thomson-Shore, Inc. is a member of Green Press Initiative, a nonprofit program dedicated to supporting authors, publishers, and suppliers in their efforts to reduce their use of fiber obtained from endangered forests. For more information, visit www.greenpressinitiative.org.

Cover design by Valerie Brewster, Scribe Typography.
Text design by Rodger Moody and Connie Kudura, ProtoType Graphics.
Printed on acid-free papers and bound by Thomson-Shore, Inc.